TODAY'S WORLD

THE PLANET
EARTH

DOUGAL DIXON

SHOOTING STAR PRESS

CONTENTS

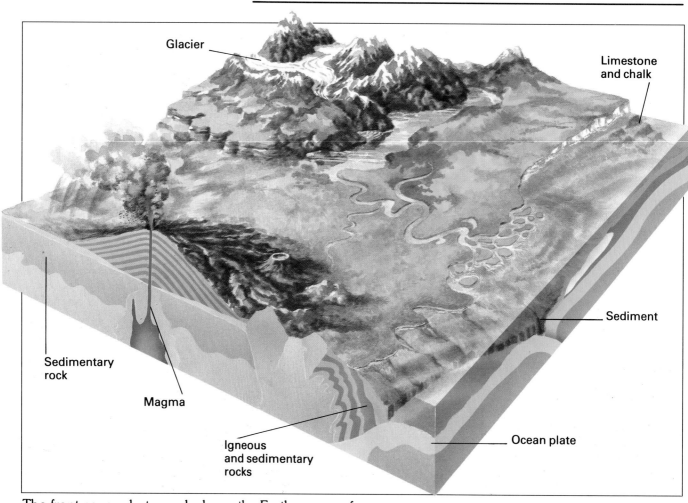

Glacier

Limestone and chalk

Sedimentary rock

Magma

Igneous and sedimentary rocks

Sediment

Ocean plate

The front cover photograph shows the Earth as seen from space.

INTRODUCTION

The Earth has always been home to the human race. But how much do we really know about this planet? The Earth is constantly altering. Some of the changes are obvious – day turns to night, spring turns to summer. These changes are caused by the Earth's rotation on its axis and by its orbit around the Sun. But deep inside the Earth, heat within the mantle is also causing structural effects to the outer skin, or crust, of the Earth.

In addition to the natural changes on Earth, there are those caused by the human race. Activities such as farming, mining and the building of towns and cities alter the face of the Earth. Pollution poisons the rivers, lakes and air – even the protective screen of the atmosphere has been affected by the release of chemicals into the air. The overall result is that much of the Earth's well-balanced ecological system is being destroyed. A better understanding of our planet – its rocks, soil, water and gases – will help us preserve the Earth for the future.

Desert sands in Algeria

ORIGINS OF THE EARTH

The Earth was formed about 4.5 billion years ago.
It is not a true sphere but slightly flattened at the poles.
Polar radius: 6,356.8 km (3,949.9 miles).
Equatorial radius: 6,378.2 km (3,963.2 miles).
Surface area: 510,100,000 sq km (196,950,000 square miles).
Volume: 1.083 trillion km^3 (260 billion cu mi).

The deepest hole ever drilled into the crust of the Earth reached a depth of 15 km (less than 10 miles). This is the merest pinprick on the surface of the whole vast globe, 12,750 km (7,900 miles) in diameter, on which we live. We have direct experience only of the rocks in the crust, the water in the oceans and the gases in the atmosphere that surrounds the Earth. What scientists know about the interior comes from indirect evidence, such as the patterns of earthquake waves as they pass through it. They can also analyze the composition of meteorites, and, assuming that they have the same origin as the Earth and everything else in the Solar System, can make certain deductions about the substances that lie inside the Earth deep beneath our feet.

Formation of the Earth

The Solar System – the Sun and planets – formed from a spinning mass of gas and dust (1). As it rotated, it contracted, and most of the material gathered in the center (2). Atomic reactions in this dense center produced the first sunshine (3). The planets were produced as the rest of the dust gathered in eddies (4). As each planet formed, the heaviest material sank to the center, leaving lighter solids, liquids and gases on the outside. Heat generated in the process produced a volcanic surface of molten rock for a time. Then, over millions of years, the surface cooled and the atmosphere changed.

Primordial atmosphere

Semi-molten surface

Volcanic activity

Oxygen and plant life

Formation of the solar system

1   2   3   4

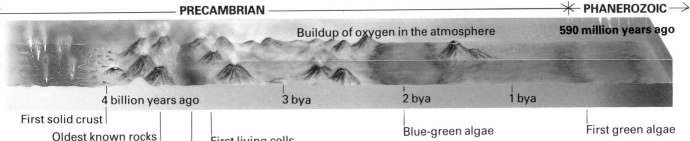

Buildup of oxygen in the atmosphere

590 million years ago

4 billion years ago   3 bya   2 bya   1 bya

First solid crust

Oldest known rocks

Continents and oceans formed

First living cells

Blue-green algae

First green algae

Geological time scale

When we talk about the age of the Earth and the various events that took place on it, we are considering vast periods of time, in terms of billions of years. Basically the history of the Earth can be divided into two main sections. The Phanerozoic covers the last 590 million years and has left a good record in the form of many fossils. The Precambrian encompasses everything before that, back to the formation of the Earth about 4.5 billion years ago. Latest evidence suggests that there has been life of some kind on the Earth for almost as long as there have been solid rocks and watery oceans to support it.

Inside the planet
If the Earth were cut across we would see that it is made up of circular layers, like layers of an onion. The behavior of shock waves from earthquakes confirms this.

Crust

The lightest material forms an outside crust a few tens of kilometers thick. There are two crustal types – a granite-like crust that forms the continents, and a heavier magnesium-rich crust beneath the oceans.

Mantle

Most of the Earth – about 82 per cent of its volume – consists of the mantle. It is a solid, silica-rich material, although there is a softer layer near the boundary with the crust.

Outer core

The only liquid layer within the Earth is the outer core, 1,820 km (1,140 miles) thick. It consists mostly of molten iron, and its constant circulation gives rise to the Earth's magnetic field.

Inner core

The solid mass, 1,600 km (1,000 miles) in radius, at the center of the Earth, is probably a heavy lump of compressed iron, with small amounts of other metals such as nickel.

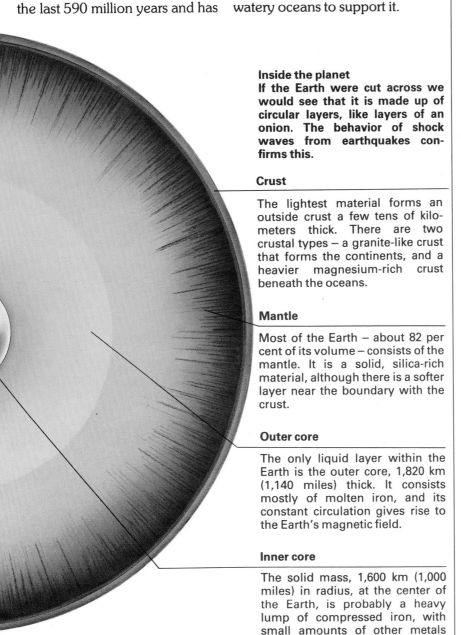

The atmosphere

The lightest part of the Earth is the atmosphere, a gaseous envelope around the outside. Light though they are, gases do have weight, so the atmosphere is compacted and densest near the Earth's surface, and gets thinner towards the vacuum of space.

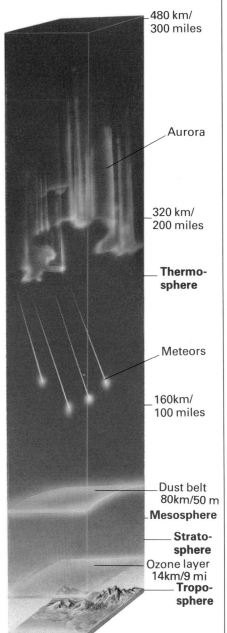

480 km/ 300 miles

Aurora

320 km/ 200 miles

Thermo-sphere

Meteors

160km/ 100 miles

Dust belt 80km/50 m

Mesosphere

Strato-sphere

Ozone layer 14km/9 mi

Tropo-sphere

LAND AND SEA

Land area: 148,800,000 sq km (57,470,000 square miles).
Total continental crust area (including continental shelf): 166,860,000 sq km (64,427,000 square miles).
Total oceanic crust area: 343,240,000 sq km (132,500,000 square miles).

A world map shows the linked continents of the Americas, the continuous sweep of Europe, Asia and Africa, isolated Australia, and desolate Antarctica sitting over the South Pole. Yet it was not always like this. Throughout time the continents, and indeed the entire Earth's surface, have been constantly in motion. The process is known as plate tectonics. It has been understood only since the middle of the 20th century, because most of the effects can be seen only at the ocean bottom. But a knowledge of plate tectonics is fundamental to an understanding of the processes that shape the Earth.

The floating continents

The Earth has two kinds of crust. Continental crust is made of granite and similar rocks. It is lighter than ocean crust which is made up mostly of the rock called basalt. As a result, the continental crust rides higher than the layers of the ocean crust, and the continents are therefore mostly dry land. They are slowly carried by the movements of the plates, like logs embedded in the ice of a frozen river. When two plates collide, the continents are never dragged down into the Earth. Instead they crumple up at the edge and form long folded mountain chains, like the Andes in South America. When two continents collide they produce a really massive mountain chain, such as the Himalayas, which were formed by the collision between India and Asia.

The Andes formed when two plates collided.

The abyss

A typical cross section of the Earth's surface shows all the features of plate tectonic movement. The plates, consisting of the crust and the topmost part of the mantle, are like floating rafts that move away from each other. The continents are carried along with them. The edges of the continents are usually awash, and the section flooded by the sea is known as the continental shelf. At a "destructive" plate margin, where two old plates meet, one plate descends and melts, usually producing molten rock that rises and erupts as chains of volcanic islands along the ocean trenches. The islands of Hawaii were formed in this way.

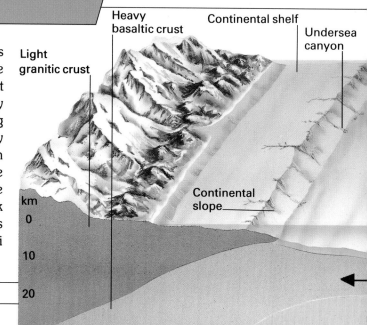

Light granitic crust

Heavy basaltic crust

Continental shelf

Undersea canyon

Continental slope

km
0
10
20
30

Ocean floor movement

The surface of the Earth is constantly on the move. New crust is being created all the time as old crust is destroyed. The surface of the Earth is made up of a number of plates, like the tiles on a floor. Each "tile" is growing along one edge and being destroyed along another. Molten material from the Earth's interior wells up between a pair of plates and solidifies into new ones, which continually move away from each other like conveyor belts. Along these "constructive" plate margins lie the ocean ridges, resembling chains of underwater volcanoes, such as the Mid-Atlantic Ridge. Where two old plates meet, one slides down below the other and is destroyed. Such "destructive" plate margins produce deep ocean trenches.

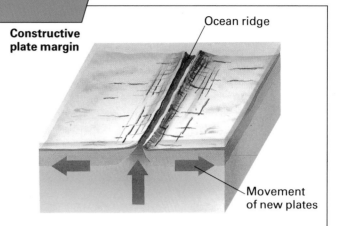

Constructive plate margin

Ocean ridge

Movement of new plates

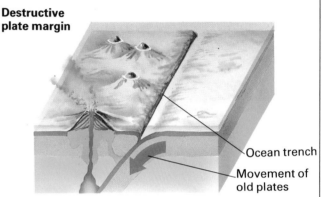

Destructive plate margin

Ocean trench

Movement of old plates

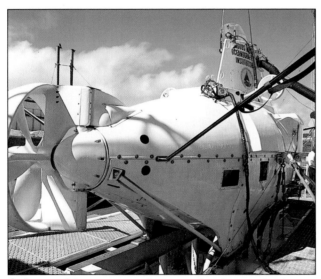

Submersibles are used to study the seabed.

Exploring the ocean floor

Submersibles are small submarines that can carry two or three people deep down in the ocean. Scientists use them to study the ocean floor, particularly deep trenches at the edges of crustal plates. One submersible descended to the bottom of the Mariana Trench, 10,920m (35,820 ft) deep in the Pacific Ocean. Some submersibles have hydraulic "arms" and "hands" for collecting samples of rock and mud.

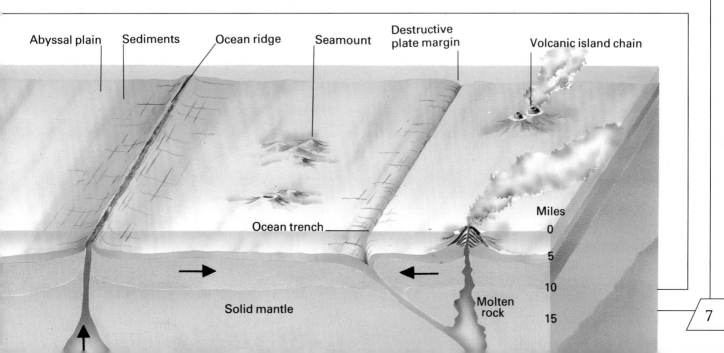

Abyssal plain   Sediments   Ocean ridge   Seamount   Destructive plate margin   Volcanic island chain

Ocean trench

Miles
0
5
10
15

Molten rock

Solid mantle

Drifting continents

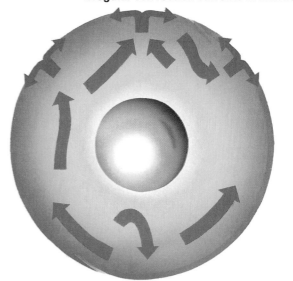

The forces that move the plates and continents on the surface of the Earth have their origins deep in the Earth's mantle (1). The heat generated at great depths produces slow-moving convection currents (see right) that churn relentlessly, millimeter by millimeter. Where the hot material rises there are volcanoes. Where it descends, it drags down the solid surface layers with it, producing a long rift valley, like the one in eastern Africa, as the continent begins to be pulled apart. Sometimes volcanoes appear where hot material forces its way through the valley floor (2). As the valley widens, the sea floods in (3) – as is happening in the Red Sea. New oceanic crust then forms between the two sections of continent, resulting in an ocean like the Atlantic Ocean.

Formation of ocean basins

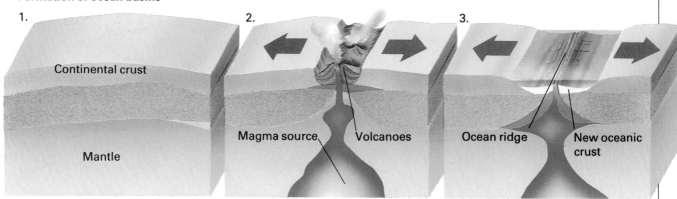

1.
Continental crust

Mantle

2.
Magma source   Volcanoes

3.
Ocean ridge   New oceanic crust

Continental drift

About 200 million years ago all the continents of the Earth had come together into one super-continent called Pangaea. Since then the various continents have separated and drifted apart. The continents are carried along until they reach a destructive plate margin, where they stop traveling, and their leading edges are crushed up into mountain chains.

By using various pieces of geological, biological and physical evidence, geologists have been able to plot the position of the continents through time. All the evidence shows that, slowly but surely, the continents are still moving.

Continental drift

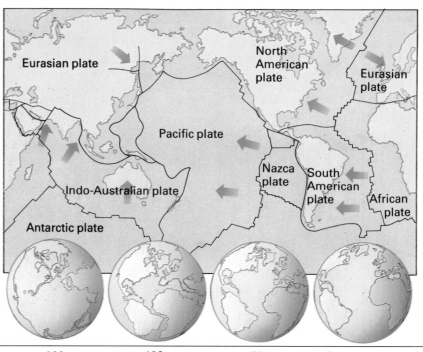

Eurasian plate

North American plate

Eurasian plate

Pacific plate

Nazca plate

South American plate

African plate

Indo-Australian plate

Antarctic plate

Millions of years ago:	200	100	50	Present day

Earthquakes are measured on two scales.
The Mercalli scale (I to XII) is a measure of intensity. It varies from place to place for the same earthquake.
The Richter scale (1 to 8) is a measure of the magnitude, and has a single value for a particular earthquake.

The movements of the plates of rock that form the Earth's crust are so small as to be imperceptible, but their effects can be readily seen at their edges. New material welling up between them, and the molten rock produced as old plates break down, can occasionally burst through to the surface. The friction produced by plate movements can release vast amounts of destructive energy. The result can be some of the most terrifying of natural phenomena – earthquakes and volcanoes – often producing damage and death on an enormous scale.

Plate tectonics

Crustal plates move at a rate of a few centimeters per year, but at their edges there can be some quite violent and spectacular effects. The upwelling of molten rock from the mantle injects new material between the edges of the plates. Some may come right through to the surface and produce underwater volcanoes. These are found all the way along the ocean ridges, but only rarely do they come to the ocean surface as in Iceland. Destructive plate margins also produce molten material that rises to the surface as volcanoes, resulting in chains of volcanic islands, such as Japan and the Philippines, along ocean trenches. It also creates volcanoes, such as Mount St. Helens in the United States, among the fold mountains of the edges of continents. Where plates move against each other they remain locked solid for many years until the tension becomes too much, and they crack and jump into the new position. This movement produces an earthquake. For this reason, the pattern of earthquakes and volcanoes around the world traces out the lines of the plate margins.

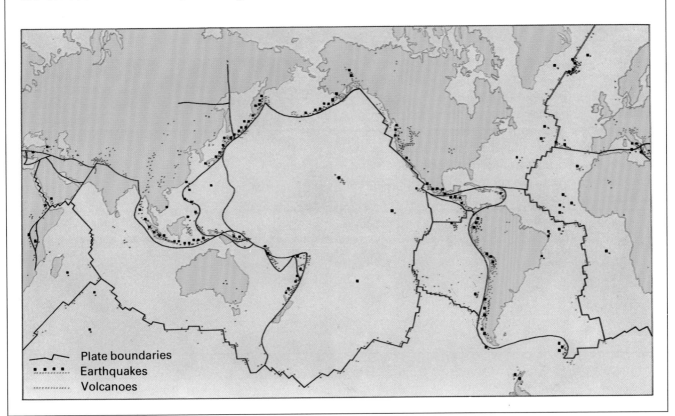

```
———⌐_  Plate boundaries
▪▪▪▪▪   Earthquakes
·········  Volcanoes
```

Volcanoes

When molten rock, called magma, erupts from the Earth's interior it cools and solidifies. On the surface the magma is known as lava, and it tends to accumulate around the fissure (a narrow opening or crack) that lets it through. Successive lava flows and eruptions of ash build up a hill called a volcano. At some volcanoes the lava consists of basalt rock and is quite runny. It can flow for long distances before solidifying, and produces broad low volcanoes, such as those in Iceland. At other volcanoes the lava is thick, slow-moving andesite rock, and it builds up high cone-shaped volcanoes. Andesite volcanoes are the more dangerous because they erupt very violently, as did Mount St. Helens in 1980.

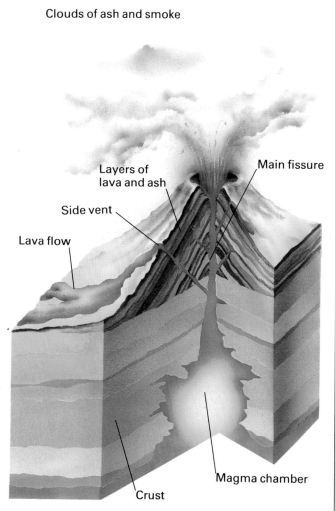

Clouds of ash and smoke

Layers of lava and ash

Main fissure

Side vent

Lava flow

Crust

Magma chamber

Molten lava pouring from a volcano

Some volcanoes erupt to the surface from an underwater ocean ridge. In the tropics a fringing coral reef forms around the volcano. As the moving plate carries the volcano away from the ridge into deeper water, the eruptions stop and the volcano sinks. But the reef continues to build upward, and a barrier reef forms around the shrinking island. Eventually the volcano submerges, leaving the reef as a growing ring called an atoll.

Undersea volcano forms island

Island submerges and coral forms

Only coral remains

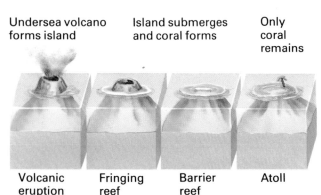

Volcanic eruption

Fringing reef

Barrier reef

Atoll

Some volcanoes erupt from under the sea.

Earthquakes

Earthquakes are produced as two sections of the Earth's crust move against each other. This usually happens at plate margins, where the continual movement builds up tension along the boundary. The time comes when the stress between the plates becomes so great that the rocks suddenly snap apart into new positions. The energy released sends shock waves for long distances through the rocks, causing the ground to shake and shudder. The point at which the greatest movement takes place is called the focus of the earthquake. The point on the surface immediately above is called the epicenter. The main shock is usually followed by aftershocks, as the rocks settle into their new positions.

Earthquakes can cause extensive damage to roads and buildings.

A seismograph records earthquake shock waves.

Earthquakes are studied by means of a seismograph. A huge weight suspended from a bar remains stationary as the rest of the instrument and the whole building it is in shakes with an earthquake. The relative movements produce a trace on a revolving drum. One earthquake can be recorded by several seismographs around the world. By comparing the timings of the shock waves, geologists can locate the earthquake's focus.

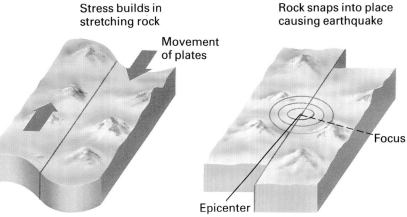

Plates slide against each other

Stress builds in stretching rock

Movement of plates

Rock snaps into place causing earthquake

Focus

Epicenter

A fold that bends the rocks upward is an anticline. A fold that bends the rocks downward is a syncline. Faults are left- and right-lateral, depending on which way the opposite block has moved: normal if the block has moved downward, reversed if it has moved upward.

The hills, valleys, mountains and chasms of the Earth – its topography – have their origins in the relentless movements of rocks in the Earth's crust. Plates colliding with each other force their edges to crush and crumple into long chains of fold mountains. At the edges of other plates the continental masses are torn apart, with depressions and rift valleys subsiding between the moving blocks. Molten material (or magma) that is churning deep in the crust, blisters up the rocks of the surface, contributing to the varied landscapes of our planet.

Fold mountains

When two crustal plates collide, one slides down beneath the other. The overriding plate may carry a continent, and this becomes deformed at the edge and shot through with volcanic material rising from below. The sediments on the descending plate are scraped off and plastered to the edge of the continent, producing further ranges of mountains along the coast. The rocks that are deformed are bent up and twisted, like layers of cloth. But the structures are not usually seen as rounded hills, because their tops are being constantly worn down by erosion as the mountains rise. The world's mountain chains – the Rockies, Andes, Alps and Himalayas – are still forming in this way. The Russian Urals, Scottish Highlands and American Appalachians formed in this way in times past.

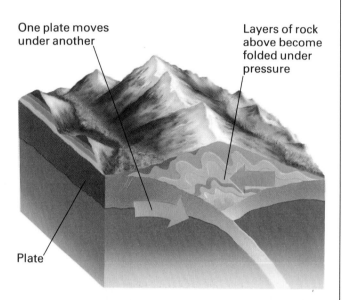

One plate moves under another

Layers of rock above become folded under pressure

Plate

The Himalayas are fold mountains that formed where continental plates collided.

Block mountains

When a mass of rocks cracks, and the two sections move, the movement produces a geological structure called a fault. Faults can be on a very small scale, or they can stretch the length of a continent. The San Andreas Fault in western North America marks the boundary between the Pacific and North American plates.

In eastern Africa, the vertical motion of faults produces mountains and valleys. A new plate margin beneath the continent is pushing that side of the landmass upward into mountains, while the tensions are allowing long blocks to subside into rift valleys. Folding and faulting often occur together. The pressure that produces fold mountains may also split them into faulted blocks and slide them over each other.

A rift valley in northeast Africa

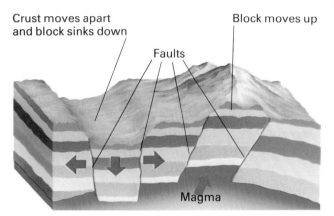

Crust moves apart and block sinks down

Block moves up

Faults

Magma

Rift valley   Block mountain

Dome mountains

Molten material welling up from deep below the Earth's surface is usually less dense than the rocks through which it passes. It often stops rising when it reaches a level where the rocks are of the same density. The new rock may then collect at this level in a massive magma chamber. Less dense fluid generated in this chamber may later burst its way to the surface as a volcano, but usually the chamber grows quietly at depth. As it fills and grows it may push up the rock layers above, bowing them up into dome mountains such as the Black Hills of South Dakota.

Eroded peaks in the Black Hills of South Dakota

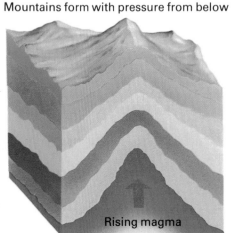

Mountains form with pressure from below

Rising magma

Magma pushes rock up from beneath

There are two types of igneous rock: acidic, rich in silica (such as granite), and basic, low in silica (such as basalt).

The three types of sedimentary rocks are clastic, from fragments (sandstone), chemical, from precipitation (rock salt) and biogenic, from living material (coal).

There are two types of metamorphic rocks: thermal, from heat (marble), and regional, from pressure (slate).

Minerals are the building blocks from which rocks are made, and the rocks are, in turn, the building blocks of the Earth. A mineral is a substance with a particular chemical composition that is formed by natural processes in the Earth, and it often forms in a crystalline shape. A rock usually has only a few types of minerals. There are three types of rock. Igneous rock forms when molten material, such as magma or lava, cools and solidifies. Sedimentary rock forms from sediments – sands, muds and rubble – that have gathered on the bed of the sea or a river and have been compacted and cemented together into a solid mass. This process takes millions of years to take place. Metamorphic rocks are formed from either igneous or sedimentary rocks that have been cooked and compressed to such a degree that new minerals have grown in them.

Elements

When the Earth formed, most of the heavier elements sank to the core. As a result, the Earth's crust consists mostly of lighter materials. Oxygen is the most abundant element in the crustal rocks, followed by silicon. Consequently most of their minerals are compounds of oxygen and silicon, with or without other elements, and are called silicates. The rocks of the continental crust tend to be made of silicates of aluminum, whereas the rocks of the ocean crust tend to be made of heavier silicates of magnesium or iron.

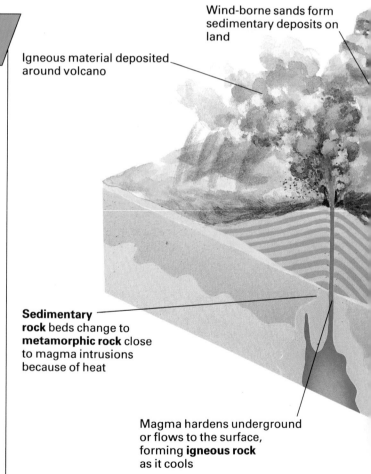

Wind-borne sands form sedimentary deposits on land

Igneous material deposited around volcano

Sedimentary rock beds change to **metamorphic rock** close to magma intrusions because of heat

Magma hardens underground or flows to the surface, forming **igneous rock** as it cools

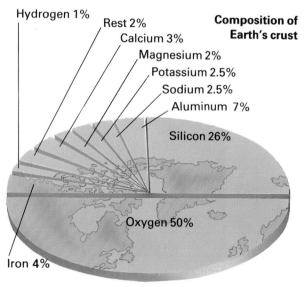

Hydrogen 1%
Rest 2%
Calcium 3%
Magnesium 2%
Potassium 2.5%
Sodium 2.5%
Aluminum 7%
Silicon 26%
Oxygen 50%
Iron 4%

Composition of Earth's crust

How rocks are formed and broken down

Rocks are being constantly destroyed and renewed in a process that is known as the rock cycle. Igneous rocks may form as coarse crystalline masses underground, like granite, or as lava from volcanoes on the surface, like basalt. These and all the other rocks, when they are exposed to the air, crumble into rubble and dust.

The rock fragments are washed down by rain, glaciers and rivers and collect as sediments in deserts, in river beds or on the bottom of the sea. There they are covered and compressed by more sediments. Water, seeping through the sediments, deposits minerals that cement the particles together. The results are sedimentary rocks such as conglomerate from pebbles, sandstone from sand, and shale from mud.

In cliffs and sides of gorges, various kinds of sedimentary rock can be seen as bands or layers. At great depths these rocks may become so compressed and heated that the mineral content sticks together and new rocks form – the metamorphic rocks, such as gneiss and marble.

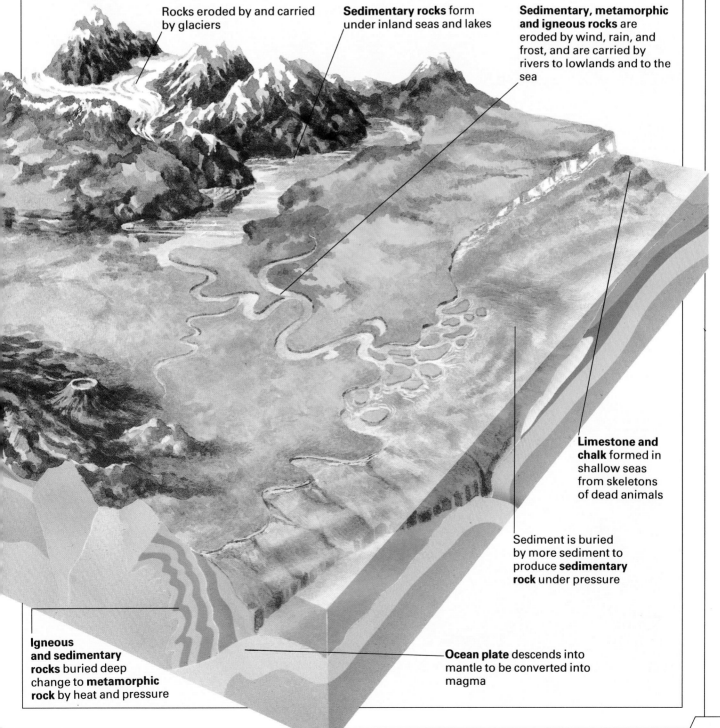

Rocks eroded by and carried by glaciers

Sedimentary rocks form under inland seas and lakes

Sedimentary, metamorphic and igneous rocks are eroded by wind, rain, and frost, and are carried by rivers to lowlands and to the sea

Limestone and chalk formed in shallow seas from skeletons of dead animals

Sediment is buried by more sediment to produce sedimentary rock under pressure

Igneous and sedimentary rocks buried deep change to metamorphic rock by heat and pressure

Ocean plate descends into mantle to be converted into magma

THE EARTH'S RICHES

Most ores and precious minerals – mineral resources – are found in mountainous regions. Other minerals, such as salt, are found dissolved in the water of lakes and seas. Even gold occurs in sea water, but it is too costly to extract it.

To most people, the word "minerals" is used to describe useful substances that can be dug out of the ground. The Earth's crust is made up of about 3,000 minerals. An economic mineral is one that can be put to some use and so has some economic or strategic value. Very few of the Earth's minerals are valuable in this way, and those that are must be found in great enough concentrations and quantities to make them worth mining. The economic minerals, apart from fossil fuels, fall into three main categories. These are ore minerals, gemstones and chemical and building materials.

Ore minerals

Most valuable metals exist as minerals in rocks. But they are usually in the form of silicates, and cannot easily be removed from the mineral. Most ore minerals are compounds of metals with oxygen or sulfur (oxides or sulfides) or are even found as the pure metal. They are mined where they have been concentrated by one of several natural Earth processes. Ore particles are often heavier than other minerals and may form distinct layers at the bottom of cooling magma chambers. Some may be dissolved from the rocks by water, and then be deposited as veins in cracks. Heavy minerals eroded out of the rocks may be washed to a corner of a riverbed and piled up there, or even washed up in distinct bands on a beach.

An open-cast copper mine in Montana

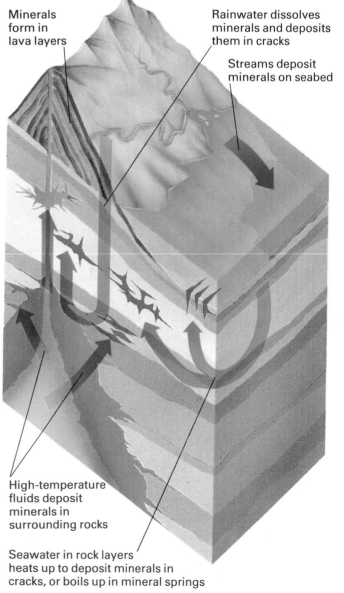

Minerals form in lava layers

Rainwater dissolves minerals and deposits them in cracks

Streams deposit minerals on seabed

High-temperature fluids deposit minerals in surrounding rocks

Seawater in rock layers heats up to deposit minerals in cracks, or boils up in mineral springs

Precious minerals

A gemstone is a mineral that, because of its purity and beauty, is highly prized and valued, especially when cut and polished as jewelry. Diamond is the most prized gemstone, made of crystallized carbon that has been brought up from close to the Earth's mantle. Ruby, amethyst and sapphire are forms of the mineral corundum – a hard oxide of aluminum. Emerald and beryl are varieties of a beryllium and aluminum silicate. These are usually deposited in veins from igneous masses. Jade is a metamorphic mineral, a silicate of sodium and aluminum. Opal, agate and onyx are non-crystalline varieties of the mineral silica. Most gemstones are found as individual crystals in veins, or in igneous or metamorphic rock.

All these gemstones are forms of corundum.

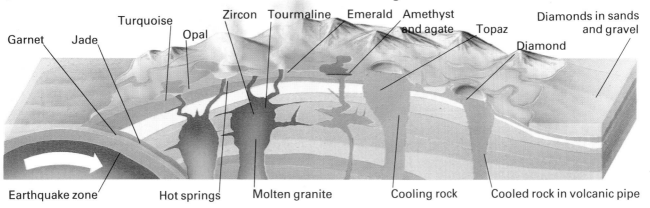

Garnet Jade Turquoise Opal Zircon Tourmaline Emerald Amethyst and agate Topaz Diamond Diamonds in sands and gravel

Earthquake zone Hot springs Molten granite Cooling rock Cooled rock in volcanic pipe

Other minerals

There are certain other minerals, apart from metal ores and gemstones, that are economically important. Building stone is an obvious example, and can include limestone, sandstone and granite for building blocks, and slate and thinly bedded sandstone for roofing. Fine clay minerals are the basis of potters' clay and ceramics. Minerals that form raw materials for the chemical industry include sulfur, deposited from volcanoes, and nitrates, precipitated into ancient lake bottoms. Mica, a silicate mineral that forms in thin paperlike crystals, is used for electrical insulation. Asbestos is a silicate material that forms fibrous crystals, and it can be spun and woven as a textile. Asbestos was once employed as a heat insulator, but it is no longer used because of the threat to health from breathing in the fibers.

Sulfur on rocks in a volcano crater

Wood contains 49.65% by weight of carbon; the rest is mainly hydrogen, oxygen and nitrogen. As it changes into coal, the carbon content increases. Peat contains 55.44% carbon, lignite 72.9%, bituminous coal 84.24% and anthracite 93.50%. Anthracite is the best fuel but is usually difficult to mine.

Much of today's energy comes from the remains of things that died millions of years ago. Plants trap the energy of the Sun and use it to make food from carbon dioxide gas in the atmosphere and water and minerals in the soil. The carbon of the carbon dioxide is used, and the oxygen is given off. When a plant dies it decomposes – the oxygen of the air turns the carbon back into carbon dioxide, and the energy is released again. Coal and oil come from plant matter that did not have a chance to decompose; the energy remains trapped in it until it is burned.

Coal

Coal is the carbon of ancient wood that has not rotted away. Normally wood decays and the carbon in it oxidizes into carbon dioxide (with the energy produced being released into the atmosphere). Sometimes, however, if trees are growing in a swamp, they may be covered by mud as soon as they fall. This seals the wood from the air and it does not decay. As time goes on, the wood becomes compacted, and the carbon becomes more and more concentrated. As this process continues the wood may become peat, lignite (brown coal), bituminous coal and finally anthracite. When any of these is burned, the carbon is oxidized to carbon dioxide (as should have happened millions of years ago), but this time the heat energy can be harnessed and put to good use.

Men cutting peat in Scotland

Peat
The first stage of the formation of coal occurs when dead swamp vegetation piles up as a fibrous brown substance called peat.

Lignite
After burial for several millions of years, the peat may become a form of soft brown coal called lignite.

Bituminous coal
At great depths and after prolonged burial, the lignite becomes the familiar black glossy bituminous coal.

Anthracite
Heat and pressure may change the coal into the metamorphic rock called anthracite – the most valuable coal of all.

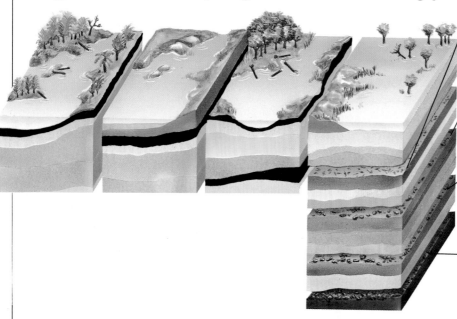

Oil and gas

The most valuable and sought after of today's fossil fuels is oil. It probably formed from masses of floating animals and plants (plankton) that sank to the sea floor at depths where there was no oxygen to oxidize the organic matter. However, some scientists believe that it actually formed as a by-product of the formation of metamorphic rocks. Whatever its origin, it lies as a fluid in the pores of certain rocks – the source rocks. If the rocks are permeable – that is, if the pores are connected to each other like a sponge – the oil can move. Because oil is lighter than water, it always tends to float above any ground water that is in the rocks, and so it rises. Eventually it may come to a layer of rock that is not porous – called a cap rock. If there is no way around this cap rock, the oil accumulates there, filling all the pores in the rocks beneath. A structure that gathers oil like this is called a trap. Engineers can penetrate the cap rock with drills and pump out the crude oil, or petroleum.

Extracting oil and gas in the North Sea

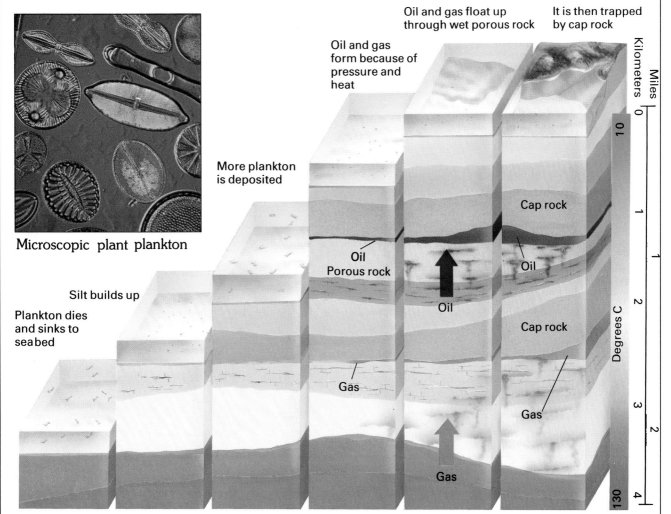

Microscopic plant plankton

Plankton dies and sinks to seabed

Silt builds up

More plankton is deposited

Oil and gas form because of pressure and heat

Oil and gas float up through wet porous rock

It is then trapped by cap rock

Oil
Porous rock

Oil

Gas

Gas

Cap rock

Oil

Cap rock

Gas

Miles
Kilometers

Degrees C

0

1

2

3

4

0

1

2

10

130

Agriculture, the first stage of civilization, started 10,000 years ago. The human population is increasing at a greater and greater rate. From AD 1 to AD 1500 it doubled; now it is doubling every 40 years. There are more people alive now than the total number of all who have ever lived before. At the end of the 1980s there are 5 billion people on the Earth.

Everything that happens on our planet has an influence on everything else. Energy is absorbed from the Sun. This heats the Earth's spherical surface and the atmosphere, and determines the Earth's climate zones. The climate has an influence on the type of vegetation that grows in a region and the kinds of animals that live there. The growing plants keep the atmosphere rich in oxygen, allowing animals to breathe. Animals keep up the levels of carbon dioxide needed for the plants to exist. The circulation of air around the globe goes hand in hand with circulation of moisture, and determines which areas are rainy and which are deserts. In all of this the human population must find its place. A small disturbance of any part of the well-balanced system may eventually have serious and unforeseen consequences somewhere else.

The energy systems of the Earth go in cycles. Moisture circulates around the oceans, the atmosphere and the land. Oxygen circulates between plants and animals. Raw materials are extracted from the environment by people, used, and eventually returned to the environment as waste or pollution.

Pollution of the Earth

All industry has waste products of some sort. Power stations produce carbon dioxide and soot. Raw materials must be refined and the components that are not used have to be dumped. When goods wear out, they are more often thrown away than repaired and used again. All in all, there is a vast amount of rubbish and waste that is put back into the environment every year, and this is called pollution.

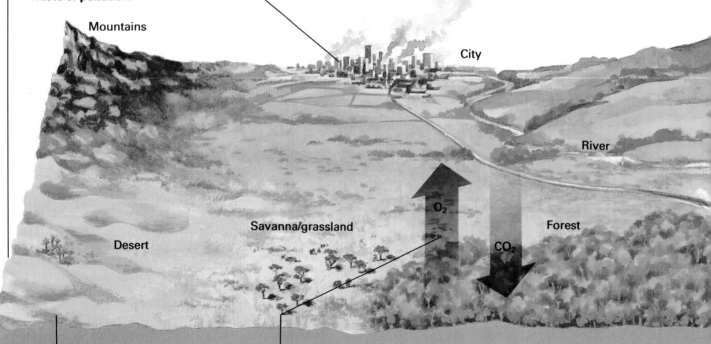

Mountains

City

River

Forest

O_2

CO_2

Savanna/grassland

Desert

Climatic zones

Air heated by the Sun in the tropics circulates northward and southward. Different climates occur at different latitudes.

Oxygen cycle

Plants use the energy of the Sun to make food from carbon dioxide (CO_2). This releases oxygen (O_2) into the atmosphere. Animals breathe in the oxygen and breathe out carbon dioxide, and when they die they decompose to carbon dioxide, all of which helps to feed the vegetation.

Studying Earth from space

Since the middle of the 20th century there has been an increasing use of "remote sensing" to find resources, to forecast weather and to monitor the effects of changing environments and pollution. Many different kinds of satellites can be used to photograph the Earth's surface. Infrared photography shows the Earth in false colors, but the colors can be interpreted to show healthy (and unhealthy) crops, the location of mineral deposits, or the distribution of water or something similarly useful.

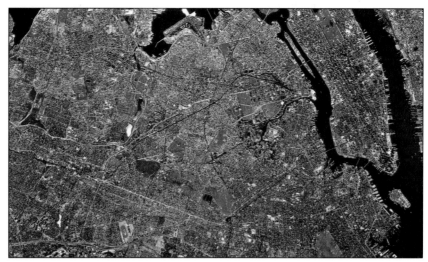

Vegetation is red on this infrared photograph of New York City.

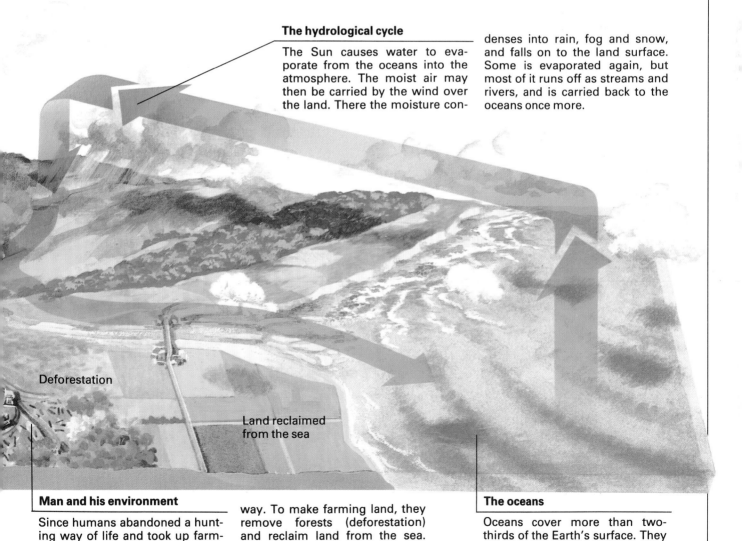

The hydrological cycle

The Sun causes water to evaporate from the oceans into the atmosphere. The moist air may then be carried by the wind over the land. There the moisture condenses into rain, fog and snow, and falls on to the land surface. Some is evaporated again, but most of it runs off as streams and rivers, and is carried back to the oceans once more.

Deforestation

Land reclaimed from the sea

Man and his environment

Since humans abandoned a hunting way of life and took up farming and industry, they have been altering the environment in some way. To make farming land, they remove forests (deforestation) and reclaim land from the sea. They cover great areas with buildings in which to live and work.

The oceans

Oceans cover more than two-thirds of the Earth's surface. They are the reservoir of all our water, and stabilize coastal climates.

Earth's coldest place is Vostok, Antarctica; average temperature of −57.8°C (− 72°F), coldest recorded −89.2°C (−128.6°F). **The average hottest place is Dallol, Ethiopia**, at 34.4°C (94°F). **The highest temperature ever recorded was at Al' Aziziyah, Libya**, at 58°C (136.4°F).

Climate and weather are not the same thing. Climate is the total pattern of all the atmospheric effects – including sunshine, rainfall, temperature and so on – regarded over a long period of time. Weather, on the other hand, describes the day-to-day variations within this expected pattern. Climate is ultimately caused by the amount of sunlight reaching an area – because this causes convection currents in the atmosphere and generates the prevailing winds – and the closeness to the sea – because this supplies moisture and can modify the harsher effects of the temperature.

Climatic zones

The varying climate around the Earth can be divided into a number of zones. In a band straddling the Equator there is constant hot Sun. This makes the air rise, and brings in wet winds from the north and south. The hot wet conditions produce an equatorial belt of tropical rainforest. The hot air that rises at the Equator spreads northward and southward, cools, and descends over the tropics. This air is now dry, and so there is a belt of desert along each tropic. Between the tropics and the Equator the conditions vary from very wet to very dry, as the Sun moves north and south in the sky with the seasons. Grasses can withstand these conditions, and tropical grasslands thrive in these zones. In high latitudes, heavy cold air from the poles produces cold desert conditions, or tundra. Where the cold polar air and warm tropical air meet, there are temperate conditions giving rise to coniferous forests in the cooler regions and deciduous forests in the warmer areas.

■ Coniferous forest		□ Grasslands	Ice cap
▨ Deciduous forest		▨ Desert	
▨ Rain forest		▨ Tundra	

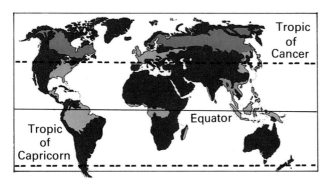

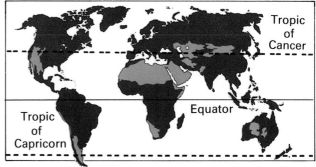

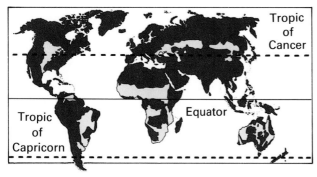

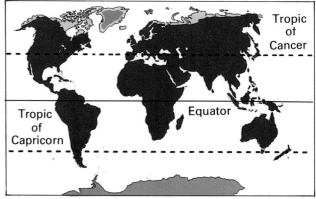

Air movements

The constant circulation of the air forms a distinctive pattern over the globe. Hot air rises at the Equator, spreads northward and southward and then descends. Cold air descends over the poles and spreads toward the tropics. These movements give rise to characteristic "cells" of air circulation. At ground level, the lower arms of the cell produce the prevailing winds. Trade winds converge on the Equator, whereas westerlies blow just out of the tropical area. Turbulent conditions form in temperate latitudes where warm and cold air masses meet. But winds do not blow due north and south. The turning of the Earth deflects them to the right and to the left.

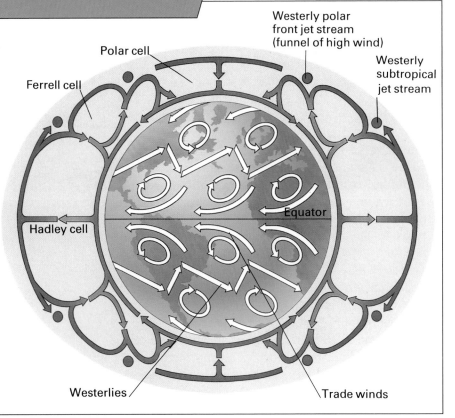

Westerly polar front jet stream (funnel of high wind)

Westerly subtropical jet stream

Polar cell

Ferrell cell

Equator

Hadley cell

Westerlies

Trade winds

Seasonal changes

The Earth's axis of rotation is tilted at an angle of 23.5°. As a result, at one time of the year the North Pole is pointing away from the Sun and six months later it is pointing towards it. This produces the seasons of winter and summer, with spring and autumn in between. As the Earth goes around the Sun, the climatic zones move north and south with the seasons. When the North Pole is pointing towards the Sun, the hottest area is along the Tropic of Cancer. When it is pointing away from the Sun, the hottest area is in the Southern Hemisphere, along the Tropic of Capricorn.

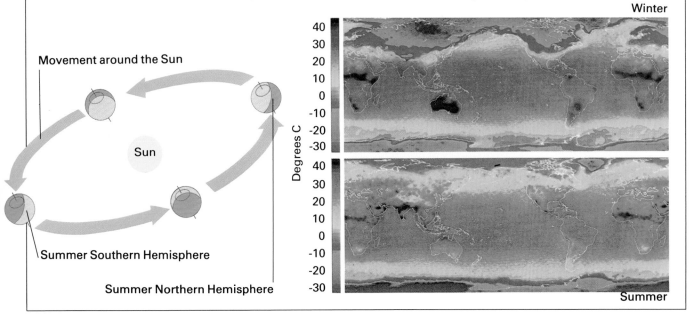

Movement around the Sun

Sun

Summer Southern Hemisphere

Summer Northern Hemisphere

Winter

Summer

Degrees C

40
30
20
10
0
-10
-20
-30

40
30
20
10
0
-10
-20
-30

Stormy weather

A hurricane is a small, intense low-pressure area that may form in the tropics. Heated air rises very swiftly, drawing in winds from all around it. Because of the turning of the Earth on its axis, the winds move in a spiral toward the center, and then swirl upward with great force. The air in the hurricane is moist and forms distinctive cloud types. Close to the surface are spiral strings of lumpy "cumulus" clouds. Toward the center these become the towering dark "cumulonimbus" thunderclouds as the air is swept upward. At the top the water turns to ice as the winds spread out again and produce high feathery "cirrus" clouds. Usually the first sign that a hurricane is approaching is the appearance of cirrus clouds in the sky. At the center of a hurricane is the "eye" – a cloudless region of calm with the fury of the hurricane raging about it. This whole system may move slowly westward, with clouds that produce torrential rains and winds that can cause much damage on exposed islands and east coasts. A hurricane can be 500 km (more than 300 miles) across, and is easily spotted from space. A miniature version, called a tornado, sometimes causes damage in North America.

An Atlantic hurricane, photographed from space

Cross section of a hurricane

High-level cirrus

Cumulus and cumulonimbus

Cumulonimbus

Large cumulus

Small cumulus

Cold air rushes in

Eye

Warm air spirals up

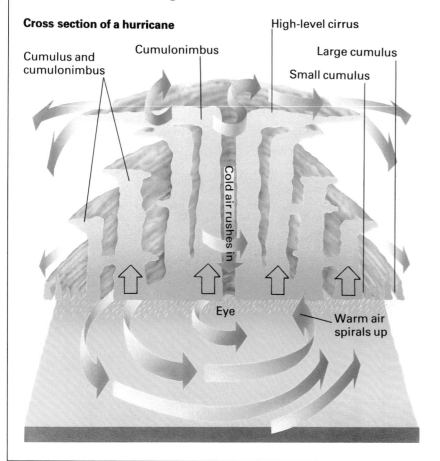

A tornado sucks up a funnel of dust

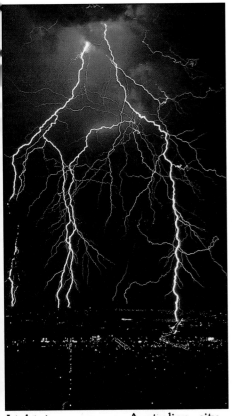

Lightning over an Australian city

The weather is so important in our everyday lives that forecasting has become an important science. Reports of conditions at weather stations scattered over a large area are drawn together to produce maps of the weather at particular times. These are analyzed to see how the conditions are likely to change in the short term and the long term. Computers can now help with this work. Much weather forecasting folklore is based on the appearance of clouds. At a "front," where warm air meets cold air and rises over it, the different types of cloud can show the movements of the different air masses (see diagram, bottom).

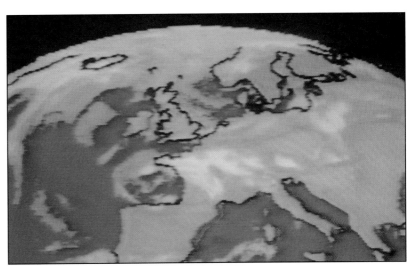

Computer-drawn map used in weather forecasting

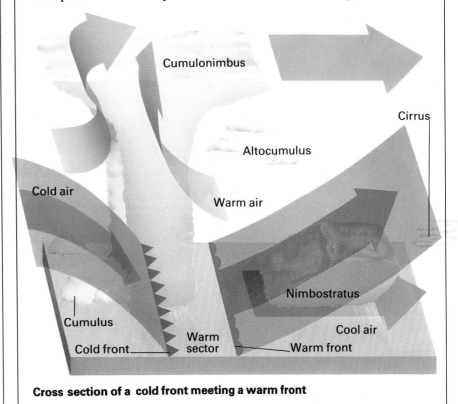

Cumulonimbus

Cirrus

Altocumulus

Cold air

Warm air

Cumulus

Nimbostratus

Cold front

Warm sector

Cool air

Warm front

Cross section of a cold front meeting a warm front

97% of the Earth's water is contained in the oceans. The total volume of seawater is 1.35 billion km³ (334 million cubic miles). Seawater contains dissolved salts at a concentration of between 33 and 38 parts per thousand; sodium and chlorine together make up 86% of these.

When seen from space our planet appears as a blue ball, with multicolored patterns of continents scattered upon it. Patches of cloud resemble white tufts of cotton. But it is the ocean that is the most obvious feature from a distance. This is hardly surprising, because more than 70 per cent of the Earth is covered with water, and it fills in the hollows between the upstanding masses of continental crust. This vast volume of water is constantly moving, whether pulled into tides by the gravity of the Moon and the Sun, or thrown into waves and pushed along as worldwide currents by the winds.

Restless sea

The waters of the ocean are in constant turmoil. The winds blowing across the surface drag the water particles along and whip them up into waves. On a larger scale the prevailing winds generate great currents across the ocean surface. The converging winds at the Equator drive the equatorial currents westward, and these then spread north and south as warm currents along the eastern edges of continents. The movement of each current continues eastward in cooler latitudes, and then returns towards the Equator as a cold current. This whole circulation gives a rotating pattern called a gyre, each gyre typically occupying half an ocean. Westerly winds (winds blowing from the west) drive a cold circumpolar current in the continuous seaway that surrounds Antarctica.

The major ocean currents

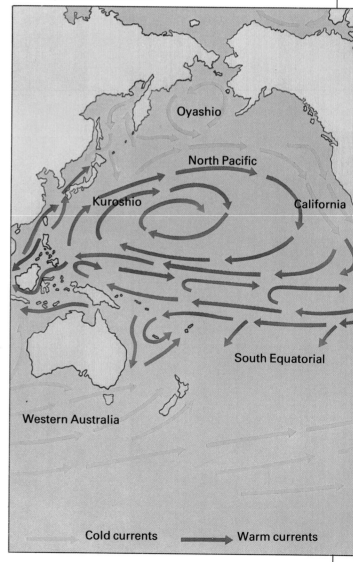

Oyashio

North Pacific

Kuroshio

California

South Equatorial

Western Australia

Cold currents   Warm currents

Wind-blown waves crash on a rocky shore.

Seawater

The winds drive the waves on to the shore, where they surge up beaches and pound against cliffs. As a wave approaches a headland it swings around and attacks it from the side. The cliffs there become undercut and are continually worn back. Caves are worn out along cracks and zones of weakness in the rock. If the caves at each side of a headland meet in the middle, they may form a natural arch. Eventually, as the arch enlarges, the top of it collapses, leaving the offshore part as an isolated stack.

Eventually the headland is destroyed, and the rocky debris formed is pounded to sand by the waves and distributed along the beaches. When waves approach a beach at an angle, the sand and pebbles are also washed up at an angle. As the wave withdraws, the fragments are washed straight down the slope, to be carried up at an angle by the next wave. This continuous movement is called "longshore drift" and it gradually moves the sand and pebbles along the beach in one direction.

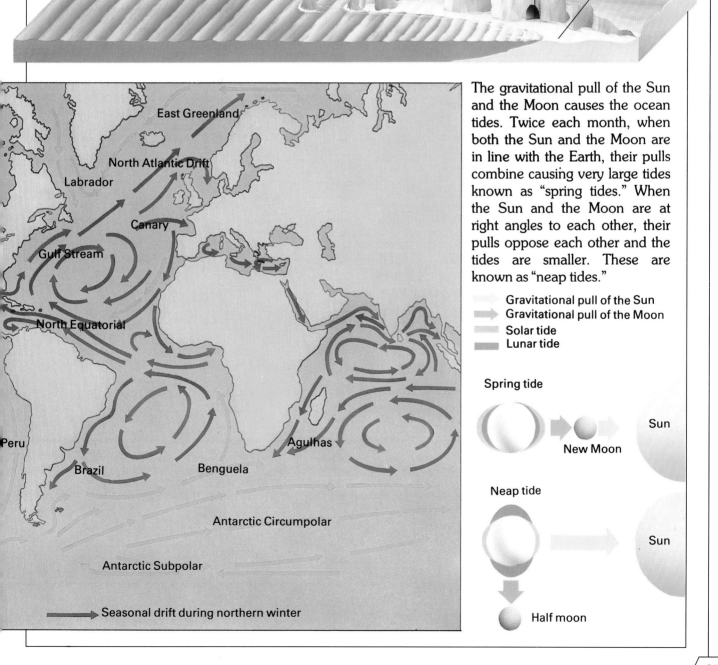

The gravitational pull of the Sun and the Moon causes the ocean tides. Twice each month, when both the Sun and the Moon are in line with the Earth, their pulls combine causing very large tides known as "spring tides." When the Sun and the Moon are at right angles to each other, their pulls oppose each other and the tides are smaller. These are known as "neap tides."

Gravitational pull of the Sun
Gravitational pull of the Moon
Solar tide
Lunar tide

RIVERS AND LAKES

Only 34% of the Earth's water is outside the oceans. About 75% of this water is ice; most of the remainder is ground-water. Rivers and lakes contain only 0.33% of all non-ocean water, and river water has only 0.2% of the saltiness of seawater.

The tiny part of the Earth's water supply that is not held in the oceans is either locked up as ice or is taking part in the water cycle. Water is evaporated from the oceans by the Sun's heat. It then falls as rain on the land, where it gathers to form streams and rivers, and eventually returns to the oceans. Water also trickles through the rocks, and can form lakes and ponds in the hollows. Nearly all the water that is used by humans, whether for drinking, watering crops, use in industry or generating power, is caught somewhere in this part of the cycle.

River profile

A river may begin as a spring that feeds a stream in the hills or mountains. There the water may drop from crag to crag and splash downward in narrow gullies as it races to the lowlands. This is known as the youthful stage of the river's life. Stones carried by the river wear away the stream bed and cut downward, carving out deep gorges that are typical of mountain rivers. On leaving the mountains the river reaches its mature stage. Now it has widened and flows more slowly. The valley is wide and winding. The bed and the banks are still being eroded, but some of the heavier transported material is dropped, usually on the insides of curves. In its old age the river ceases to erode. It meanders slowly across a flat plain, depositing debris as it goes. A vertical section of the river's course, showing its steep youthful stage and its flat old age stage, is called the river profile.

A fast-flowing river provides sport for canoeists.

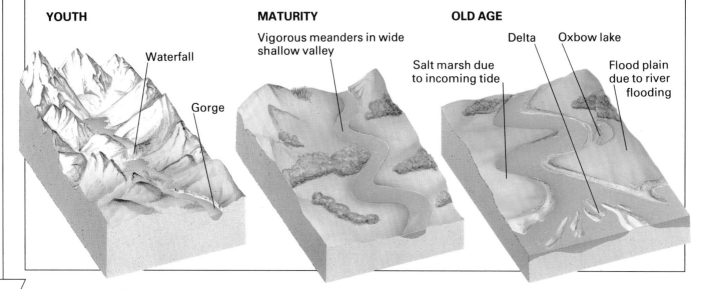

YOUTH

Waterfall

Gorge

MATURITY

Vigorous meanders in wide shallow valley

OLD AGE

Delta

Oxbow lake

Salt marsh due to incoming tide

Flood plain due to river flooding

Springs and watersheds

Water falling as rain may run off or soak into the ground. The water that soaks in accumulates when it reaches a layer of non-porous rocks, and the soil and rocks above this level become saturated. The upper limit of this saturated zone is called the water table. When the slope of a hill cuts across the water table, the water seeps out and forms a spring. Usually there is a line of springs along a hillside at a certain level – the springline. A range of mountains usually has springlines at each side, so that all the streams and rivers flow away from the mountain crest. The line that runs along the crest between the springlines is called the watershed, and it divides one river basin from another.

A mountain river cascades over a waterfall to the valley

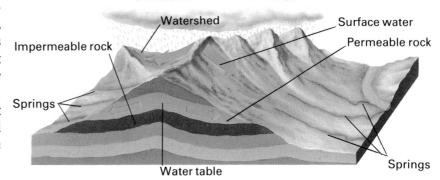

Lakes and reservoirs

Natural hollows tend to fill up with water to form ponds and lakes. Many lakes are in areas that were covered with ice during the last Ice Age. Glaciers are heavy, and they gouge out deep hollows in the bedrock as they move. Once a glacier melts, the hollows fill with water. Such glacier lakes are found throughout lowland Canada, and at the heads of the glaciated valleys in the mountains.

Freshwater lakes are useful stores of water. Today many of them are artificial, having been created by engineers. The easiest way to do this is to build a dam across a valley, and then let the valley fill up with river water. Such reservoirs can be used for drinking water, for irrigation of agricultural land or for providing a flow of water that can turn turbines to generate electricity.

Lake Titicaca, the world's highest lake

An artificial lake behind a dam in Canada

WASTELANDS

A desert can be defined as any area that has less than 30 cm (12 inches) of rain in a year. The greatest daily temperature range was recorded in the Sahara, from 52°C (126°F) in the day to 2°C (36°F) at night. Ice caps cover 15,600,000 sq km (6,050,000 square miles) of the Earth's surface.

There are certain places on our planet where conditions are so harsh that it is impossible, or at least very difficult, for life to exist. These include the coldest and the hottest places on Earth. All of these desert wastelands have one thing in common — their dryness. Water is essential for all living things to live and grow. If conditions are so cold that all the water is frozen as ice, or if the conditions are so hot that all the water has evaporated, then the result is an uninhabitable wasteland. In a hot desert all the year's rain may fall in just a few days. In a cold desert any moisture falls as ice and snow.

Ice sheets

Some places are so cold that nothing lives there, neither people nor anything else. The poles are two such areas. At each end of the Earth's axis the Sun is never high in the sky. In fact, within the Arctic and Antarctic Circles, there are times during the year when the Sun never rises at all. Temperatures are so low that water is present only as ice. And because most biological processes are based on water, it is hard for life to exist. In other ways, however, the two areas are quite different. The North Pole is in an area of frozen sea. In the lands around it, life does flourish in the brief summer. The South Pole, on the other hand, lies in the middle of a continent which is covered by broad glaciers forming a permanent ice cap.

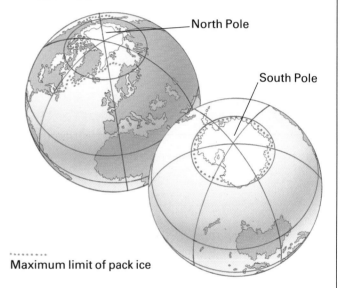

North Pole

South Pole

.... Maximum limit of pack ice

A massive iceberg floating in the Antarctic Weddell Sea

Glaciers

A glacier is a river of ice. Snow gathering in a mountain valley and piling up year after year becomes compacted to ice. Under the pressure of gravity this ice can slowly flow like putty, and the whole mass moves downhill. The ice on the surface is still brittle and breaks into crevasses and pinnacles caused by the movement beneath.

During the Ice Age there were more glaciers than there are now. As they moved downhill, their great weight deepened and widened their valleys, grinding them into a distinct U-shape. Now that such glaciers have melted, the U-shaped valleys show where they once flowed. The rocks that have been scraped away are spread over the lowlands.

A glacier high up in the Swiss Alps

Pasture in an Alpine valley in Austria

Deserts

Deserts occur where very little rain falls. This may be along the tropics where dry air descends, as in the Sahara and the Kalahari. Or it may be in the lee of a mountain range, sheltered from any moist wind – for example, California's Death Valley. Or it may be too far from the sea for rain to reach, as in the Gobi Desert in Asia. Some deserts are by the sea, like the Namib in Africa, but no rain falls because of the pattern of winds over the area.

A desert is dry and hot by day. But at night the temperature often drops to freezing because there is no insulating cloud cover. Rocks expand and contract with the change in temperature. Whatever moisture they contain forces the pores apart and they crumble to sand. Dry winds hurl sand about, polishing and wearing away exposed rock faces. Some deserts are covered in sand, some with rubble, and others consist of disintegrating rock.

Winds blow the sand into dunes in a desert.

Rocky desert landscape in Utah

THE HUMAN FACTOR

The world's largest excavation is Utah's Bingham Canyon copper mine. It has an area of 7.2 square km (2.8 square miles) and is 774 m (2,500 ft) deep.
The Dutch have been reclaiming land from the sea since the 7th century.
One-third of the world's forests have been chopped down.

The Earth is our home. We need it to give us the food we eat, the raw materials for industry, and the spaces in which we live and enjoy ourselves. But populations are increasing all the time, and every year we make more and more demands on our planet. Two hundred years ago it would not have had much effect if we had cut down a forest to produce enough farmland to feed a city. Today if we did the same thing, it would do untold damage to the dwindling forest areas of the world. Increasing populations make increasing demands on the environment.

Human settlements

People have always needed space in which to live. When populations were small this had little effect on the environment or the landscape. Roman towns, for example, were small and compact. Now, however, with world populations increasing explosively, more and more land must be taken up just for living space. Industrial cities were originally built close to the site of their raw materials, such as iron ore deposits or coal seams. Canals were built to bring in the raw materials that were not close by, and to carry away finished goods. The factories and the homes of those who worked in them were always side by side. Nowadays, with improved communications and transport, the factories can be far from their raw materials, and workers can travel to them from quite a distance away.

Many early cities grew up alongside rivers.

Athens, the capital of Greece, has modern buildings close by ancient ruins.

Land and desert reclamation

In many low-lying areas, such as the Netherlands, fresh land is being reclaimed from the sea. This is done by enclosing a shallow sea area with a series of dykes. The dykes are made from two rows of boulders and clay, with sand in between. This gives a sturdy dam, and the seawater contained behind the dyke can be pumped out and the land can be used for farming.

The opposite effect is needed for reclaiming desert areas. In cases such as these, water must be brought in from elsewhere. Often river water is channeled into the desert area by the use of dams and canals. In other instances a well is drilled into a deep bed of rock that contains water. In Israel, certain desert areas have been reclaimed and successfully converted for fruit-growing.

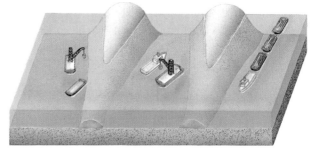

Barges dump two parallel rows of mixed boulders and clay alongside each other

Dredged sand is pumped into the gap and a road built on top

Reclaimed land

Irrigation can make fertile fields in deserts.

Sea is pumped out to reclaim the land

Misuse of the Earth

Civilization and technology take their toll on the Earth. Mountains are ripped away for raw materials, forests are cut down for farmland, and waste products pollute the rivers and seas, poison the air and spoil the landscape. Steps are being taken to reduce the effects. National parks, reserves and other restricted areas are set aside and all of these activities are forbidden. Farmland should be managed properly so that it does not become worn out after a few years. Raw materials should be conserved and, if possible, waste products should be recycled or turned into by-products and used efficiently. It is important to remember that the Earth's spaces and resources are not infinite.

National parks aim to preserve wildlife.

MAPPING THE EARTH

The Earth is a sphere. Mapmakers therefore have a problem representing its surface, because it is impossible to represent a curved surface accurately on flat paper. Whenever a map of the world is shown, there is always distortion somewhere.

There are a number of different ways, or projections, to show the world. The one below is an equal-area projection that shows the land masses in relation to each other. But to achieve this, the directions and the shapes have been distorted. Other projections can show directions correctly, but distort the areas of the continents and oceans. Some can show the true shapes of the countries but distort directions and areas. Each map has to be made using the projection most suitable for its purpose. One concerned with area needs an equal-area projection, one used for navigation must not distort directions.

A globe is the most accurate map of the Earth.

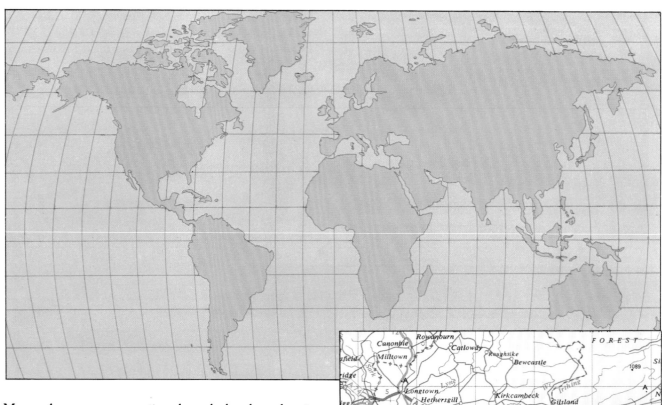

Mapmakers use conventional symbols when drawing up a map. Contours are lines that join points of equal height, and are used to show hills and valleys. Different colors of roads are used to denote their width. Little pictures may be used, such as tents showing camping sites. Various types or sizes of printing are also significant – some kinds of letters show towns or counties, some farms, others ancient monuments, and so on. By using a system of defined symbols, a mapmaker can include a wealth of information on a single map.

GLOSSARY

Antarctic Circle Line of latitude of 66.5°S, south of which the Sun does not rise for at least one day of the year.

Arctic Circle Line of latitude of 66.5°N, north of which the Sun does not rise for at least one day of the year.

Atmosphere Envelope of gases that surrounds the Earth.

Basalt Dense fine-grained igneous rock; low in silica.

Epicenter Point on the Earth's surface directly above the focus of an earthquake. It is usually where most of the damage occurs.

Equator Line of latitude of 0°. It lies midway between the North and South Poles.

Erosion Breakdown and wearing away of rocks on the Earth's surface by water, waves, glacial ice, wind or other natural forces.

Fault Crack in the Earth's crust, along which displacement occurs.

Focus Point within the Earth's crust at which the greatest motion of an earthquake takes place.

Fold Deformation of rock strata by bending.

Granite Light-colored, coarse-grained igneous rock that is high in silica.

Gyre Large-scale circulating cell of ocean water composed of two or more currents.

Igneous rock Rock formed when a mass of molten material cools and solidifies.

Lava Molten rock that erupts at the Earth's surface from a volcano.

Longshore drift Movement of sand and pebbles along the seashore, driven by the action of waves.

Magma Molten rocky material below the Earth's surface.

Mantle The part of the Earth's structure, rich in silica, that lies between the core and the crust.

Metamorphic rock Rock formed when pre-existing rocks are altered by heat or pressure but without melting (otherwise the result would be an igneous rock).

Meteorite Piece of rock of extraterrestrial origin (a meteor) that has fallen to Earth.

Ore Mineral that contains metal which can be extracted and used.

Phanerozoic Period of geological time from 590 million years ago onward, from which there is a good fossil record.

Plate tectonics Movement of the Earth's surface by the formation and destruction of "plates" made of the crust and the uppermost part of the mantle.

Precambrian The period of geological time before 590 million years ago, from which there is no good fossil record.

Projection Means of showing the curved surface of the Earth as a map. The theory is that if a light is placed at the center of a hollow world globe, it projects a shadow pattern of its surface features on to a surrounding cylinder, cone or flat sheet and the resulting pattern is the basis for a map.

Reef Ledge of rock or coral at or near the surface of the water.

Rift valley Valley formed as a block of Earth's crust subsides between two faults.

Sedimentary rock Rock formed from loose material deposited (usually under water) in beds, and solidified by compaction and cementation by minerals.

Silica Abundant substance consisting of an oxide of silicon; its commonest form is sand. Combined with other elements, it forms silicates, which make up most of the minerals in the Earth.

Strata (singular stratum) Beds or layers of sedimentary rock.

Supercontinent Very large continent formed when several continents are brought together through the action of plate tectonics.

Tide Movement of the world's seas caused by the gravitational forces of the Sun and Moon.

Topography A region's landscape features – mountains, valleys, plains and so on.

Tornado Violently rotating column of air a few meters in diameter that may occur at fronts over continental areas.

Tropic of Cancer and **Tropic of Capricorn** The two lines of latitude (23.5°N and 23.5°S) between which the Sun is directly overhead at some time during the year.

Vein A mineral-filled crack that cuts across other rock structures.

Water table Level below which all pores and cracks in rocks are saturated with water.

INDEX

All entries in bold are found in the Glossary

Photographic Credits:
t = top, b = bottom, l = left, r = right
Cover and pages 11 (b), 19 (b), 24-25, 25 (l and r) and 30: Science Photo Library; intro page and pages 10 (b), 11 (t), 17 (b), 26, 28, 29 (l) and 31 (bl and br): Spectrum; pages 10 (t), 12, 21, 24 (b), 29 (r), 31 (tl and tr), 32 (t), 33 (b) and back cover: Robert Harding; pages 7, 13 (b) and 16: Bruce Coleman; pages 6, 13 (t), 32 (b), 33 (t) and 34: Hutchison Library; page 18: Survival Anglia; page 19 (t): ELF; page 23: U.S. Weather Department.